GOOD GROOMING FOR GIRLS

Good Grooming

FOR GIRLS

♀

by Rubie Saunders

illustrations by Anne Canevari Green

Franklin Watts
New York / London / Toronto / Sydney / 1989

Revised Edition

Library of Congress Cataloging-in-Publication Data

Saunders, Rubie.
Good grooming for girls / by Rubie Saunders ; illustrated by Anne
Canevari Green.—Rev. ed.
p. cm.
Bibliography: p.
Includes index.
Summary: An introduction to personal hygiene and grooming for
girls, including tips on cleanliness, hair styling, diet, and
makeup.
ISBN 0-531-10769-8
1. Grooming for girls—Juvenile literature. 2. Beauty, Personal—
Juvenile literature. [1. Grooming. 2. Beauty, Personal.
3. Health.] I. Green, Anne Canevari. II. Title.
RA777.25.S28 1989
646.7′042—dc19 89-30963 CIP AC

To my niece
Nicole

Photographs courtesy of:
Randy Matusow: pp. 10, 45;
Monkmeyer Press Photos:
pp. 16 and 29 (Michal Heron),
40 (Elizabeth Hibb),
54 (Renate Hiller),
57 and 70 (Sybil Shackman),
71 and 75 (Mimi Forsyth),
78 (Arlene Collins),
86 (Sybil Shackman);
Photo Researchers: pp. 22
(Richard Hutchings), 36
(Maureen Fennelli), 66 and
87 (Spencer C. Grant III);
USDA: p. 62.

Contents

GOOD GROOMING FOR GIRLS

*Good grooming means being
healthy, fit and clean.*

GOOD GROOMING IS FOR EVERYONE

Why do some girls always look great? Is it because they have a lot of money to spend on clothes? Or maybe you think they were born knowing exactly what to wear when. The fact is, every girl can look her best all the time without having a new wardrobe every season, and it isn't a talent you have to be born with. All you need to know are the basics of good grooming, and any girl can learn them.

Good grooming is the art of looking your best on all occasions, and that isn't as difficult to master as you might think. It doesn't cost a great deal of money and you don't have to spend hours a day at it. Grooming isn't really a big thing, but it can help you to make the most of your good points, play down your "bad" points and give you the self-confidence and self-respect that everyone needs.

Dressing correctly for the occasion is an important part of grooming. But good grooming doesn't mean you have to be dressed up every waking moment; the girl who goes to a picnic in a party dress is making the same grooming mistake as the one who goes to a nice restaurant in dirty jeans.

Good grooming really begins with cleanliness. When your body is clean from head to toe and your clothes are clean and fresh, you don't have to worry about your appearance and can concentrate on making friends, on your school work, on having fun and the other activities in your busy life. And when you feel good about yourself, you make a good impression on everyone you meet.

FACE
FRONT

Your face probably seems to you to be the most important part of your appearance. You worry because it isn't perfect—your nose looks too big; your lips are too thin or too full; the shape is all wrong. But look closely at the women in your family, in your neighborhood, at school, on television and in magazines. You'll discover that few, if any, have perfect features. Besides, ideas of what constitutes a perfect face often change from generation to generation and the most attractive faces often don't fall into specific categories. The best approach is to make the most of the features you like, and don't worry about the rest. Instead of bemoaning your large nose, concentrate on your beautiful eyes. Don't fret about freckles; be grateful for your blemish-free skin.

To start with your face, keeping it clean is the first step in good grooming. The skin on your face—as well as the skin that covers your entire body—needs to be washed frequently and thoroughly. It's made up of two main layers: the epidermis, the outer layer, which itself consists of outer layers of dead cells and inner layers of live cells (the skin is constantly reproducing itself); and the dermis, the under layer. Blood capillaries, nerve endings, hair follicles, sweat glands and sebaceous (oil) glands are found in the dermis. The pigments that determine the color of your skin—melanin and carotene—are produced by skin cells in the epidermis.

By the way, the color of your skin has nothing to do with its texture. Some black girls may have skin that's more sensitive to the burning rays of the sun than some white girls; acne, oily skin, dryness are problems for everyone. So whether you're white or black, Native American, Hispanic or Asian, the care of the skin is the same.

Washing your face properly doesn't take a lot of time, and it's a habit you should develop now; it's also one part of your beauty routine that you should never neglect.

Morning and bedtime are essential face-washing times, and—unless your skin is dry—it's also a good idea to give your face another washing after school. Wash again after any strenuous activity that makes you perspire freely.

Just splashing water on your face isn't washing. To do the job right, wet your face with warm

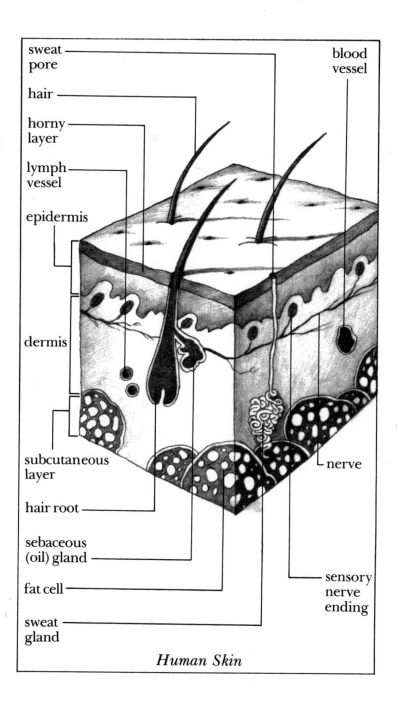

sweat pore

hair

horny layer

lymph vessel

epidermis

dermis

subcutaneous layer

hair root

sebaceous (oil) gland

fat cell

sweat gland

blood vessel

nerve

sensory nerve ending

Human Skin

Skin care starts with soap and water.

water. There's more to your face than your cheeks. Don't forget your forehead, chin, nose and throat. With a very soft washcloth or your fingers—wash your hands first, if necessary—massage soap all over your face, paying particular attention to the area around your nose and under your lips. Be sure to wash from your hairline back to your ears and down to your throat. Rinse the soap off completely, again using warm water. If you're worried about getting soap in your eyes, here's a tip: don't squeeze them shut—that only forces the soap in. Just close your eyes normally.

You can use any mild face soap, but avoid deodorant soaps and those with heavy perfumes because they tend to dry the skin. Scrubbing too hard or washing too often can also dry out your skin. If your face looks flaky or feels tight and dry after washing, switch to another soap; the one you're using may not be right for your skin. Try washing only twice a day and wash more gently.

If your face is very oily, and that's not uncommon when you're in your teens, you might want to use an astringent after washing. Astringents are usually alcohol-containing liquids that can help to dry up excess oil. You might find an astringent useful in very hot weather, or after exercising. If you try one, be careful not to get your skin overly dry.

If you have acne—and about 98 percent of girls and boys between the ages of about ten and twenty-four or so do—you may want to use a medicated cleanser after washing with soap, or even

[17]

instead of using soap. They're usually creams or lotions; apply them like soap by massaging them into your face and then rinsing them off. But to get the best results from astringents or cleansers, follow the directions. If you're unsure which product to buy, ask your pharmacist or a doctor who specializes in skin care (dermatologist).

The preteen and teen years are an oily-skin time for most of you, but some may discover that while there's a lot of oil around the nose and under the lips, the cheeks are dry. This is not uncommon; it's certainly nothing to worry about. You don't have to use two type of cleansers, either. Any cleanser or soap will do a good job on both dry and oily areas of your face if you use it correctly.

While almost everyone has acne at some time or another during the teen years, not everyone has it to the same degree. Mild cases can be treated with over-the-counter medications. These are usually vanishing creams that disappear into your skin, so they can be worn during the day as well as at night. However, serious cases need the attention of a dermatologist; see your doctor.

Acne isn't caused by dirty skin, nor is anything you eat the culprit. During puberty, the sebaceous glands produce oil faster than it can be secreted through the pores, which are tiny holes in both the epidermis and dermis layers of your skin. The pores become clogged and infection sets in. That's why washing is so important; it gets rid of that excess oil and a clean skin is much less likely to become severely infected. Drinking plenty

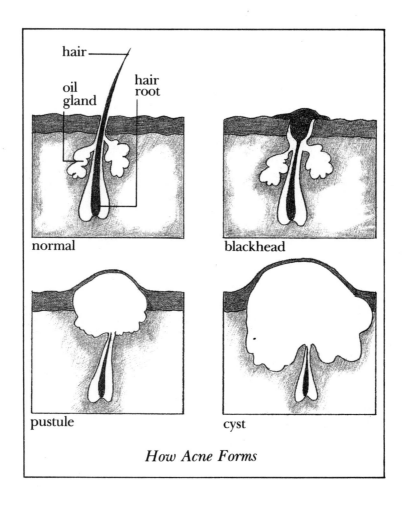

hair

oil gland

hair root

normal

blackhead

pustule

cyst

How Acne Forms

of water and fruit juices, and eating green leafy vegetables will also help your complexion.

Except when applying medication to your face or washing it, keep your hands off. Squeezing pimples can lead to permanent scars, and unwashed hands may spread infection. And you probably don't need to use special creams and lotions except for an acne condition. Moisturizers and other face creams you see advertised are for older women whose skin has lost much of its natural moisture. Except for washing, young faces are best left alone.

While thinking about your face, don't forget your teeth. Brushing regularly—in the morning, at night, and after meals when possible—and using dental floss to clean between your teeth and along the gum lines, and seeing a dentist twice a year are the essentials of good grooming for your teeth.

RUB-A-DUB-DUB

Okay, your face is clean, but what about the rest of you? Even though you may be covered by clothes from the neck down, it's essential to keep your whole body clean. Being clean all over does more than help you to look your best; it's necessary for your health, too. A small cut on clean skin isn't much of a problem, but on unwashed skin it can become infected and lead to serious trouble.

How often should you bathe? The answer is, every day. You have sebaceous glands all over your body which produce more oil than ever from the time you're about ten or so until you are in your late teens or early twenties. Your perspiration has a stronger odor then, too. That's why a daily bath or shower is so important, especially at your age. You have to get rid of the oil, stale perspiration and dirt that accumulate on your skin every day.

Being clean all over helps
you to look your best.

It doesn't matter whether you take a bath or a shower; the main thing is to go over every inch of your skin with soap and water. Use a nail brush to scrub elbows, knees, feet and other places where dirt is ground into your skin. A long-handled brush can help you scrub your back. The water should be comfortably warm. If you like a cold shower, that's fine, but use warm water for washing and cold for rinsing. Most soaps lather more in warm water, so you'll achieve better results from a warm bath or shower than a cold one.

It really doesn't matter whether you shower before bedtime or in the morning. What's important is that you take a bath or shower at least once every twenty-four hours. If you like the luxurious feeling of a bubble bath, go for it! Just remember the products that dissolve away a bathtub ring also dry up much-needed skin oils, so limit those to once a week or so. The rest of the time you'll just have to wash away that bathtub ring.

If you're devoted to showers, you may not know that sitting in a tub of warm water does more than get you clean; it relaxes you and soothes away petty problems as you wash away the day's accumulation of dirt. So, for a change, treat yourself to a relaxing half hour in the tub. On the other hand, if you're strictly a tub bather, try an invigorating shower once in a while. Standing under running water can pep you up and make you feel ready to face the world again!

But once you're in the tub or under the shower, do you know how to get yourself really clean all over? Start by washing your face as previously described. Then soap your hands or a washcloth and scrub your neck, back and front. Now wash your arms, paying particular attention to your armpits. Next come your chest and back. You'll do a good job on your back if you use a long-handled brush or a washcloth. After soaping the cloth, hold it at opposite corners with one hand over your shoulder and the other behind your back. With up-and-down, side-to-side movements, you will be able to cover your entire back. To rinse, just slip down in the tub or stand under the shower.

When you're taking a bath, you'll have to kneel or stand up in the tub to do a good job from your waist to your knees. Don't be afraid to wash the pubic area thoroughly; it needs it, and mild bath soap won't cause a problem if you rinse it away completely.

Finally, wash your lower legs and feet. Don't forget to use a brush or to scrub hard with a washcloth on your heels and knees. And be sure to wash between each toe!

Rinsing thoroughly is as important as washing thoroughly. Most soaps, even mild ones, have a tendency to dry the skin, and while your skin may be oily, you don't want to leave any trace of soap on it. If your bath water is too soapy to do a good job of rinsing, let it drain out and run in a small amount of fresh water. Rinse the soap from your washcloth and use it to remove all traces of soap from your pubic area.

Incidentally, you can—and should!—bathe or shower when you have your menstrual period. The water should be neither very cold nor very hot; it should be comfortably warm. Even if you are a confirmed bather, you may find a shower is more convenient during that time of the month. Put on a fresh sanitary napkin or insert a tampon immediately after your shower or bath and you'll be clean and fresh all over.

After drying yourself completely, you may want to apply a good body or hand lotion to your feet; it will keep them soft and smooth. Body powder also helps to prolong your freshness, especially in warm weather. You can use one that's scented or one that's also a deodorant powder.

Whether you bathe or shower, remember that clean water is precious; don't waste it. You don't have to let the shower run while you search for a clean towel or that elusive nail brush. And you certainly don't have to fill the tub practically to the top to take a bath.

HAIR CARE

Do you know that hair is hair? Whether it's thin, thick or coarse, straight, wavy, curly or kinky, that stuff growing out of your head has the same chemical components regardless of your racial or ethnic background. Like skin, every type of hair needs the same kind of care.

A pleasant old saying states that a women's crowning glory is her hair. But that's not true of oily, snarled tresses that look like a hair style for the Wicked Witch of the West. No matter what style you choose, no matter how long or short your hair is, it will look much better when it's clean. So an important item on your good-grooming agenda is regular shampooing. And that brings up the question of how often you should wash your hair. It really depends on the type of hair you have;

the oilier it is, the more frequently it should be shampooed. City girls may have to shampoo more often than those who live in rural areas.

Most girls from about ten or twelve discover that their hair has become quite oily. Once-a-week shampoos aren't enough to keep their hair looking its best. Some girls are afraid to wash it more often; they've heard frequent shampoos may damage the hair. Fortunately, that's not true. You can wash your hair every day with a mild shampoo without hurting it in any way. Frequent shampoos will help to keep your hair looking its best, and those extra washings may also help to combat an acne problem. After all, your hair often brushes your face; if it's dirty, it will aggravate any complexion problem you may have.

The best way to decide how often to shampoo your hair is by touch, look and smell. If it feels oily, wash it. If it hangs limply and is dull, wash it. If it has a sour odor, wash it. But don't wait until it's oily, limp and sour-smelling to shampoo your hair. It's better to wash it one day early than one day late. In general, even dry hair needs to be shampooed at least twice a week.

You can use any kind of shampoo you want; just remember that its main function is to get your hair clean. If it also adds bounce or a sheen or if it makes combing snarls out easier, fine, but first and foremost it should clean your hair. There are shampoos for oily hair, for dry hair and for normal hair. Some claim to be made for hair that's been permed or colored; others are for hair that's regularly blown dry. Read the labels carefully and pick one that promises to do what you want it to.

Buy the smallest size available and try it. If you are satisfied with the results, the next time buy the larger, more economical size. If you don't care for that brand, try others until you find the one that works best for your hair.

Conditioning rinses are another hair-care product you may want to try. Some are spray-ons, some are lotions, some are foams. Some claim to add body or shine or both; some are formulated to help unsnarl your hair after shampooing. Decide what you want a conditioner to do and buy one that suits your needs. Again, start with a trial size. And read the label carefully! Some conditioners are to be left in the hair; most need to be washed out after a couple of minutes. If you don't follow the manufacturer's directions exactly, you can't expect the promised results.

Should you shampoo your hair in the shower or at the bathroom sink? It really doesn't matter as long as you wash it properly. It may be easier to shampoo long hair in the sink and short hair in the shower. Some people prefer to shampoo their hair at the bathroom sink, apply a conditioner, then shower to rinse the hair completely. But the choice is yours; just be sure to get your hair thoroughly clean.

You have your shampoo and conditioner within reach and you're ready to shampoo. But first, give your hair a good brushing. Lie face down

Two latherings of shampoo and a thorough rinsing will produce shiny hair.

on your bed with your head hanging over the side, or stand up and bend from the waist, and brush your hair forward from the nape of your neck. Do this vigorously for several minutes just before you shampoo. This brings oil, dust and dirt to the ends of your hair where they can be washed away easily.

Then wet your hair completely, using water that's comfortably warm. Put a small amount of shampoo (you don't need much!) on your hair and massage it thoroughly into your hair and scalp, using the fleshy tips of your fingers. Avoid scratching the scalp with your nails. Are you disappointed because the shampoo, which promised to give mountains of lather, isn't producing many bubbles? Keep rubbing a little longer, making sure you cover every part of your scalp and every strand of hair. Then rinse, using warm water. Apply a little more shampoo, and if you've done a good job the first time, you'll see that mountain of lather. The oil and dirt in your hair prevented the shampoo from lathering the first time. That's why you always need to apply shampoo twice.

Rinse thoroughly with warm water to remove all the shampoo. This is very important because any shampoo left in the hair will cause it to look dull and feel sticky. When the water running out of your hair is clear and your hair "squeaks" when you rub it, you'll know you've rinsed it enough. Then gradually add cold water until it's as cool as you can comfortably tolerate. Cold water does a good job of rinsing away any last traces of shampoo. Squeeze the excess water out of your hair and if you're using a conditioner, apply it according to the directions on the label.

It will be easier to untangle your hair if you comb the conditioner through before rinsing it away. This also insures that each strand is covered with the conditioner.

Don't forget to wash your comb and brush each time you shampoo your hair. The easiest way to do this is to put soap on the bristles of your brush and use it to remove the dirt between the teeth of the comb. Then use the comb to remove the loose hairs and dirt from the brush. Rinse them both and they're ready to use on your sparkling clean hair.

Setting lotions, styling mousses and gels are popular hair-care aids. Read the directions on the labels of these products carefully; using too much can result in a disaster and too little won't be effective. Generally, avoid using these products every day. They can make your hair difficult to manage if you allow them to build up. And you'll have to wash your hair more often because lotions, foams or sprays help dirt and dust cling to your hair and scalp. Actually, it's better to use these products only on special occasions rather than daily, if you use them at all. For the natural styles that are most becoming, setting lotions and mousses aren't really necessary. You can style your hair very effectively with a blow-dryer.

BLOW-
DRYING
MAGIC

You should learn how to style your hair. It saves time—you can do it at your convenience. And it saves money—you won't have to rely on a hairdresser all the time. Besides, it doesn't take much time and it's great fun to experiment with different styles.

If you don't have a blow-dryer in your house, it's worth buying one. It makes drying and styling your hair much easier and faster. For some styles, you may want to invest in an electric curling iron, too. It's imperative that you read the manufacturer's directions and precautions on these products. Many of them also come with handy booklets that show you how to get the most out of them. But never use any electrical device near water; that's inviting a tragedy! To avoid an electric shock, make

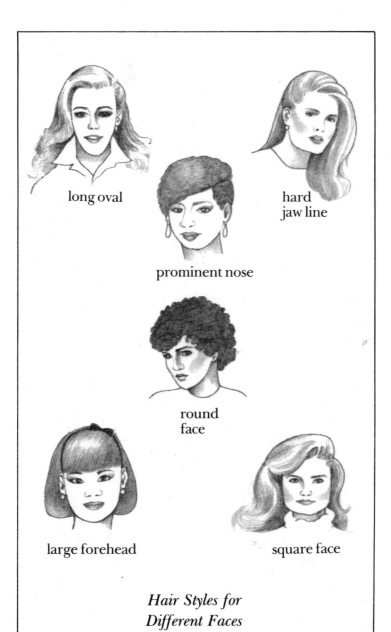

long oval

prominent nose

hard jaw line

round face

large forehead

square face

Hair Styles for Different Faces

sure your hands are dry before plugging your dryer or curling iron into an outlet.

After shampooing, towel-dry your hair until water no longer trickles down your neck. If your hair is longer than shoulder length, comb it smooth and part it in the center from front to back and across the crown from ear to ear; you'll have four sections of hair. Long hair that's also thick or very curly might need to be parted into smaller sections. Use your blow-dryer to dry one section at a time. If your dryer has a comb attachment, comb each section from scalp to ends. Move the dryer slowly through each section. Don't hold it in one place too long or you might burn your hair. Shoulder-length or shorter hair can be combed smooth and blow-dried without first being parted into sections.

When your hair is dry, use the brush attachment on your dryer to curl the ends over or under. Or you can part your hair in one-inch (2.5 cm) sections and have curls all over your head. If your dryer doesn't have a brush attachment, use an ordinary brush—not one with plastic bristles that might melt—to hold the hair in position while you blow warm air on it to set it.

Between shampoos, you can refresh your style with a curling iron or with your blow-dryer. Use a low setting since your hair isn't wet; the air from your dryer doesn't have to be very hot to style dry hair. Or you can pin your hair in place and take a warm shower to perk up your style.

Speaking of hair styles, do you know how to select one that is flattering for you? Copying the style worn by your favorite television actress or your best friend may not be the way. Experiment to see if you look best with a left or right side part, a center part or with no part at all. Does a smooth style suit you better than masses of curls? You don't have to stick to one style all the time, of course, but from one basic styling you can usually comb your hair two or three different ways.

When considering a style, you also have to give some thought to the type of hair you have.

You may admire long hair that's worn straight, but if you have very curly hair it will have to be chemically relaxed before that style works for you. Ask a reliable hairdresser about that; she or he can give you specific information about relaxing hair that has tight waves that make it hard to style certain ways. Of course, straight hair can be curled, either with a curling iron or with a permanent.

It's also important to adapt a style to suit your face. If you have a long oval face, a side part may be more flattering than a center part. The same is true if you have a prominent nose. A hard jaw line can be softened by shoulder-length hair curled at the ends. A large forehead can appear smaller by wearing side or front bangs. A curly short style is often flattering to a round face; a low side part helps a square face. Don't feel you have to follow the crowd and wear your hair exactly like everyone else. Be an individual and pick styles that are most becoming to you.

A haircut offers a chance
to try new hairstyles.

FEET
AND
HANDS

Though you wash your hands several times a day, and your feet get a good scrubbing every time you shower, you should take a careful look at them to see if they need special attention. If you're like most girls, they do need extra care.

The way your feet look and feel can be improved if you rub a good skin lotion into them every day. If the dead skin has piled up on your heels—a natural occurrence—use a pumice stone (available at low cost at drug and variety stores) to smooth it away. Remove dirt from under your toenails with an orange stick, and then use nail clippers to cut the nails straight across. This eliminates the possibility of ingrown toenails. After clipping, an emery board or nail file will smooth the edges of your toenails so they won't catch on your stockings.

If you like, you can put polish on your toenails. But stick to colors such as pink, coral, peach or natural. Blue, green, purple or dark blood-colored toenails strike many people as weird.

Sprinkling a little powder in your shoes before putting them on will make your feet feel comfortable all day. A deodorant powder is especially helpful in warm weather and if your feet perspire a lot.

You probably spend more time taking care of your hands and fingernails than your feet; after all, hands are always on view. But once you get into the habit of regular foot care, it won't take a lot of time to keep them looking and feeling great!

Of course your hands need special care, too. Use an orange stick to get out the dirt from under your nails and scrub them regularly with a nail brush. When you dry your hands, wrap a finger in the towel and gently push back the cuticle of each nail. If you do this every time you wash your hands, you won't have to use scissors to cut away the dead skin that normally builds up at the base of your nails.

With nail scissors or clippers, cut your nails straight across. Round them at the tip and smooth the edges with a fine emery board. Nails should never be cut or filed to a point unless you're playing a cat in the school play. Very long nails are a nuisance and some people think they are ugly. If you keep your nails just a fraction of an inch longer than your fingertips, they will be less likely to break and your hands will look their best.

Soap, water and a nail brush are
the basic tools of nail care.

For special occasions, you can buy paste-on nails in a variety of nail-polish shades. They're fun and are especially useful if you've broken one nail; with paste-ons all ten fingernails will be the same length.

When it comes to polishing your nails, check with Mom or Dad first. If they say okay, choose a flattering natural shade. Colorless, pale pink or rose are good selections. You might want to apply colorless or natural for every day and use the other shades for special occasions. When you buy nail polish, make sure you buy a bottle of remover, too.

To apply nail polish, wipe off the excess from the brush on the rim of the bottle and, starting just in front of the cuticle, paint a steady stroke along the side of the nail to the tip. Keep your hand steady and always work from cuticle to tip until each nail is filled in. Let the polish dry completely, then apply a second coat the same way you did the first. Each coat of polish must dry thoroughly if you want an even finish. Use a cotton swab dipped in nail polish remover to get rid of any polish on the skin around your nails.

Old or chipped polish should be taken off with remover. Don't peel it off, because that often causes the nail to peel, too. And don't cover chipped polish with a new coat; it will make the nail look lumpy. It's better to have no polish on your nails than chipped or lumpy polish.

But you don't have to wear any polish at all. Clean, well-shaped nails are quite attractive. If you bite your nails or nibble on your cuticles, polish will only call attention to your hands, so break these habits before using nail polish. Keep your hands busy playing a guitar, drawing, woodworking or whatever; you will be less likely to bite them. When you are involved in after-school activities with your friends, you'll have less time to sit around chewing on your nails. If you work at it, you can break yourself of the nail- or cuticle-nibbling habit!

If your hands are dry, apply a good hand lotion after washing and drying them. If your palms perspire a lot, rub a little body powder on them. Sweaty palms are not uncommon for young people and it's nothing to be embarrassed about. It's rarely a permanent condition, so forget about it.

CLEAN
AND
FRESH

You may have a friend who is pleasant to be near in the morning, but by midafternoon she or he smells of perspiration. This happens when a person perspires a great deal and the daily bath just isn't enough to keep her or him fresh all day long.

Perspiration has an unpleasant odor after it's been exposed to the air, and it's often a nuisance, but there are important reasons why you perspire. Skin does more than keep your insides from showing. It's the largest organ in the body and, in addition to regulating body temperature, one of its main functions is to eliminate certain body wastes. That's right; perspiration contains waste material that the body eliminates through the pores in the skin. Anyone who doesn't perspire at all may not be in good health and should see a doctor. But everyone doesn't perspire at the same rate.

[43]

If you sweat more or less than your best friend, that doesn't necessarily mean there's something wrong with either of you.

Now that you know why human beings perspire, you can understand why perspiration has a strong odor. The underarms have the strongest odor because they have a large concentration of sweat glands. Fresh sweat on a clean body doesn't have a disagreeable smell. It's the odor of stale sweat that's offensive. You don't have to put up with unpleasant body odor. After your daily shower, apply a deodorant to your underarms and you'll be nice to be near all day.

Deodorants come in many forms, including solids, roll-ons and premoistened pads. Most manufacturers have phased out deodorants in aerosol spray containers because the propellant freon has proven to be harmful to the earth's atmosphere. Then, too, inhaling them wasn't the best thing for people's lungs. There are also deodorant soaps and body powders. When you read the labels on the many different brands of deodorants available, you'll learn that some are antiperspirants as well. Try different types and different brands until you find the one that is most effective for you.

Since deodorants work with your individual body chemistry, the brand and type that works on Jessica may be totally ineffective on Nicole. You may also discover that the brand or type that worked for you when you were eleven is no longer effective now that you're fourteen. This is because

*Finding your personal style and
learning to take care of yourself
are important parts of grooming.*

your body chemistry has changed, and the formula in your old deodorant is no longer the best one for you.

Regardless of the form of deodorant you use, one thing holds true: never apply it to dirty skin. Use a deodorant immediately after your bath or washing under your arms. Deodorants are not made to remove the odor of perspiration once you have perspired. Nor are they to be used in place of your daily shower.

Deodorants prevent odor forming from perspiration without changing the amount you perspire. On the other hand, antiperspirants are designed, by means of various chemicals, to prevent perspiration under the arms. Most of today's deodorants are also antiperspirants. How effective they are depends upon how much you perspire, how your body reacts to the chemicals in them and how strong an odor your perspiration has.

You may have an allergic reaction to a deodorant. If a rash appears or the skin under your arms become sore or tender after using a deodorant, stop using it immediately. Wait until the skin is back to normal before trying another form or brand of deodorant.

Little kids don't need a deodorant, but when you're about eleven or so and your body begins to develop adult characteristics, you'll find you really need a deodorant. A good rule to follow is to start using a deodorant when you begin to menstruate or when your breasts show signs of developing, whichever comes first.

[46]

STAY
FRESH

After bathing and applying a deodorant, you might like to use cologne, toilet water or perfume to give you a longer-lasting feeling of freshness. But remember, fragrances will not disguise the fact that you haven't bathed, so use them only on clean skin. Choose a fresh floral or fruit scent and avoid the heavier, muskier fragrances. You can lightly spray (they aren't aerosols) or splash a little cologne or toilet water all over. However, perfume should be used very sparingly. It is more concentrated, and a small dab inside the wrists, at the temples and behind the ears is enough.

Along with starting to menstruate and developing breasts, another sign that your body is maturing is the growth of hair under your arms, on your legs and in your pubic area. When the hair becomes noticeable, you may decide you want to

[47]

remove it from your armpits and your legs. But don't rush to do this; shaving can be a nuisance and not everyone needs to shave these areas. Blondes, for example, may not have to shave their legs at all because the hair doesn't show. But if your hair is dark, you'll probably want to remove it.

There are several ways to remove unwanted hair. The easiest, safest and least expensive method is to shave it. But you might prefer to use a depilatory, which is a cream, lotion or foam that dissolves the hair at the skin line. Or you can strip off the hair with wax, or have it permanently removed by electrolysis.

You can buy wax hair-removing preparations at most drug stores. Read the directions carefully and follow them exactly. This method removes hair below the surface of the skin, so it takes longer for it to grow back.

Electrolysis permanently removes the hair by destroying the follicle from which it grows. This can be somewhat painful, it's expensive and the process usually has to be repeated because each hair doesn't grow out at the same time. It should be done only by a qualified professional; a dermatologist can probably recommend one in your area.

Depilatories aren't difficult to use and you don't need a razor. And they're safe as long as you follow the directions on the label exactly. Generally, all you do is smooth the lotion, cream or foam on your clean legs, wait a while and then wash it off.

Depilatories can be used under the arms as well. There are also depilatories designed to remove unwanted facial hair—especially on the upper lip. But if your facial hair isn't very heavy, you might prefer to buy a cream bleach for facial hair at a drug store. This won't remove the hair, but it will lighten it so that it's hardly noticeable. In either case, read the directions carefully and follow them exactly. Never use a razor to remove the hair on your face; it will leave unsightly stubble.

For most of you, shaving the hair from your legs and underarms is a quite satisfactory way of removing it. You can shave in the shower or in the tub. Wash your legs with warm water and work up a good lather with soap, or use a shaving foam or gel. Using a safety razor, preferably one designed for women, gently go over your legs and under your arms, removing the hair and the lather at the same time.

Rinse the razor often; if it's clogged with lather and hairs it can't do a good job. It's easy to nick yourself with a razor; don't press too hard or you'll remove some skin as well as hairs! When you're finished, rinse your legs and apply skin lotion to keep them smooth and soft. You can apply a deodorant under your arms right after shaving unless you've nicked yourself. In that case, wait a bit before applying it.

With an electric razor, you don't need any lather; the skin should be dry. Or put on a lotion especially made to be used with electric razors.

The hair on your legs and under the arms will grow back; how soon these areas need to be shaved again depends upon how fast your hair grows. But you aren't likely to need to shave every week unless your hair grows extremely quickly and is very thick.

If you want to shave your inner thigh area so no hairs show when you wear a swimsuit, you certainly can. Put on your suit so you can see exactly where the hairs show. This eliminates the possibility of shaving more than you actually need to. Cover the exposed area with lather, shave it and be sure to rinse thoroughly. Applying skin lotion to the shaved area is a good idea.

If your eyebrows are thick and straggly, you can tweeze the unruly hairs to achieve a smoother line. Don't shave the eyebrows because the skin around the eyes is much too tender for a razor. Anyway, a pair of tweezers does the job quite well. If your eyebrows grow straight across, pluck the hairs over the bridge of your nose; two brows look better than one!

WHAT
SHALL I
WEAR?

You've learned how to keep yourself sparkling clean from head to toe, but what about clothes? It makes little sense to put soiled clothing on a clean body, so learn how to take care of your wardrobe. In these days of easy-care fabrics, washing machines and clothes dryers, even a ten-year-old needn't always depend on Mom or Dad to see that clothes are laundered as often as they should be. And the oldest dress, hand-me-down jeans and secondhand shirts look much nicer when they're clean. You'll feel much better wearing them when they've been freshly laundered, too.

Good grooming, as far as clothes are concerned, starts when you shop. Whether you are allowed to buy your own clothes or whether Mom or Dad takes you shopping, you should look not only for style but also for practicality. You may see a purple shirt you just love, for example, but what do you have that you can wear it with? Will it go with your skirts and pants? If not, a yellow shirt might be a better buy.

You should get into the habit of reading the labels and tags manufacturers attach to clothing; they serve a very useful purpose. They tell you the size and price of the garment, of course, and also what kind of fabric it's made of, whether it should be hand-washed, machine-washed or dry-cleaned. Heeding this information can save you a lot of money. For example, those gorgeous white pants may be more expensive than the price tag indicates if they have to be dry-cleaned after each wearing. If that sweater you can't live without isn't available in your size, you'd be wiser to pass it by. You'll burst the seams if it's a size too small and if it's too large you'll look and feel uncomfortable when you wear it. Make a habit of reading all the tags and labels on every garment you consider buying; it can save you a lot of time and money.

While it would be wonderful to have closets full of clothes, you can manage very well with surprisingly few if you know how to choose them wisely. If you start the school year with two or three skirts, several pairs of jeans and perhaps a pair of pants, and have coordinated tops (sweaters, shirts and blouses), you can be the best-dressed girl in school if you picked your styles and colors carefully.

The art of mixing and matching tops and bottoms can make a simple wardrobe seem like a whole specialty shop full of clothes. When the colors and styles of each of your tops coordinates with your skirts and pants, you'll have a great many possible combinations to wear.

To prove this, draw a stick figure on a sheet of typing paper. Make it as large as you can. Then cut out five pant shapes, three skirt shapes and six top shapes from white typing paper. They don't have to be perfect; they only need to be rough outlines of clothes. Color in each top, pants and skirt and indicate whether it's a solid color, a print, plaid or check. Now put them on your stick figure. You'll be amazed at how many combinations you can find!

A good way to add interest to your wardrobe is by using scarves, belts and other accessories such as vests and ties. Even if you're wearing the same skirt and top you had on last week, putting a different scarf around your neck will give your outfit a new look.

You'll have less trouble keeping your clothes neat and clean if you change from your school things when you get home. Hang them up, if they don't need laundering, and when you're ready to put them on again you won't have to worry about

*The clothes you choose
reflect your taste.*

creases. If at all possible hang them outside your closet and let them air for a while before putting them away. Both the clothes and your closet will stay fresher longer if you follow this procedure. It will take only a minute or two to slip out of your nicer clothes and into an old pair of jeans and a faded T-shirt, and that's a fine outfit for listening to records or doing your homework or riding a bike to a friend's house.

There's an added bonus that comes with taking care of your clothes. When Mom and Dad realize that you show respect for your wardrobe, they may be more willing to buy you that fabulous sweater even though it costs a little more than they usually spend for such an item.

While pants are popular with girls of all ages for school, play and, in some cases, even for work, you don't have to wear them day in and day out. It's fun sometimes to wear a skirt and blouse or a dress instead of pants or jeans. And dressing up for parties or other special occasions puts you in the mood for fun; try it and see.

Coats, jackets and outer clothing do not have to be washed or cleaned after every wearing. Obviously the shorts and shirt you played tennis in are too sweaty for any place but the washing machine, but the pants you wore to school on a cool

Grooming includes taking care of your clothes, too.

day may be worn more than once. However, your bras, panties, socks and stockings should be washed after each wearing. That doesn't mean you need dozens of each, either. A half-dozen bras and panties are probably enough since they usually can be machine-washed and dried.

And remember, bras and panties are not for sleeping. Since they should be clean every day, you're not saving time by sleeping in them. It's a lazy, unsanitary practice. Besides, they're too restrictive for you to sleep in comfortably.

SMART
EATING

There's an old saying that holds some truth: you are what you eat. If you eat more food than your body needs, you'll gain weight. If you eat less, you'll lose it. But unfortunately, weight control isn't really that simple. How much food is too much? That depends upon your activities and how your body burns food. If you think you eat relatively little but are still overweight, it may be that you're eating the wrong kinds of foods. For example, a bag of potato chips and a Coke may not seem like a big lunch, but it's loaded with calories and has very little nutrition. If you have a tuna (packed in water) sandwich on thin-sliced whole-grain bread and a glass of low-fat milk, you'd have fewer calories and a lot more nutrition—and you'd probably lose weight!

If you really think you have a weight problem—you're either too fat or too thin—see your doctor. She or he is the one to tell you if you need to lose or gain weight and will prescribe a diet that's right for you. Crash diets and diets designed for adults, such as those found in many magazines, are not for you.

Regardless of whether you want to gain or lose weight, you still need proteins, carbohydrates (starches and sugars) and fats at every meal. You can seriously damage your health if you eliminate any of these basic food categories from your diet. Weight control for young teens is primarily a matter of how much or how little you consume from the essential food groups during the course of the day. And exercise is vital whether you want to add or subtract pounds.

The ideal weight for any person is determined by more than one's age. Bone structure and height are equally important factors. If you think about it, you'll realize that a girl of twelve with a small skeletal structure who's just under five feet (1.5 m) tall ought to weigh less than a girl of the same age and height who has a large frame. So don't think you're underweight or overweight because you don't tip the scales at the same weight as your best friend who is exactly your age.

You won't have to worry about your weight now and throughout your life if you develop proper eating habits. Remember those basic food groups you learned about in school? At every meal you need meat, fish or poultry or another protein source; vegetables and fruit; milk or milk products or substitutes; whether you want to gain, lose or maintain your weight. Snack on fresh fruit, raw vegetables and nuts without added salt or fats, and drink fruit juice and milk—whole, skim or low-fat—instead of candy bars, potato chips and other foods that are high in calories, cholesterol and fat. You can have them once in a while, but they should never replace a real meal or healthier snacks. Not only will you feel better, but you'll look better, too.

You don't have to be bone-thin to be attractive; actually everyone looks better with a little flesh on their bones. Don't go to the extreme and gobble everything in sight; being overweight isn't healthy. If you eat three well-balanced meals a day, increase your healthy snacks and cut down on those that provide little or no nutrition, you should never have to worry about weighing more than is healthy for you.

Eating properly means being aware of foods that are good for you and those that aren't. Be sure you are providing the protein, vitamins and minerals (especially calcium and iron) your body needs. If your diet consists mostly of foods low in fats and cholesterol such as low-fat or skim milk, very lean meat, fish and poultry, and is high in fiber-rich foods such as whole-grain bread and leafy vegetables, you're on the right track. Starches such as potatoes, rice and pasta should not be eliminated from your diet, but you can bake potatoes instead of frying them and you don't have to drown rice or pasta in sauces high in saturated fats.

*Healthy food choices are important
for you and your family.*

If you have special dietary limitations or needs, look for up-to-date nutrition guides in your library. For help with a weight-loss or weight-gain diet, look for books that stress health and fitness, not fad diets.

STRETCH
THOSE
MUSCLES

Did you know that exercise can help you to gain weight as well as lose it? It's true! When you stretch your muscles by walking, jogging, swimming or whatever, you'll improve your appetite. Just make sure you eat wisely! Actually, everybody needs to exercise; it's as important to good health—and therefore to good looks—as a healthy diet.

Take a look at yourself in a full-length mirror; how is your posture? Does your stomach stick out? Do your shoulders slouch? Is your chest sunken? Are your knees bent? Diet won't change these, but good posture will. Imagine a thin wire is attached to the crown of your head and is slowly being pulled to the ceiling. Your head comes up, your shoulders straighten, your chest expands and your stomach flattens. You look taller, thinner and much, much better.

Good posture doesn't mean standing so stiff and straight that one might think your spine is a steel rod. That is uncomfortable, and standing that way isn't attractive or good posture. Remember that imaginary wire and stand tall with your arms hanging loosely at your sides.

To keep you standing and walking straight, balance a good-sized book on your head and walk around the house. It's an old-fashioned remedy, but it really works. With very little practice, you'll be able to walk, sit and stand without making the book fall. If you practice this faithfully for about fifteen minutes a day, you'll soon discover that good posture has become a habit and you no longer need the book. Don't be surprised if friends ask if you've lost weight; you can look several pounds slimmer just by improving your posture. And your clothes will fit better, too!

You have good standing and walking posture, but how do you sit? While it's not always necessary to sit with your feet flat on the floor, your knees together, your back straight and your hands folded in your lap, you don't have to sprawl in a chair like a rag doll, either. Cross your legs if you want to, at the knee or ankles, but remember you're supposed to sit on your buttocks, not on the base of your spine.

By the way, when wearing a short skirt, keep your knees together when you sit; otherwise people can see clear up to your panties.

How do you walk? Of course, you've been getting around on your feet since you were one

*Standing and walking tall help your
health, appearance, and mood.*

or two, but dragging one foot after the other isn't really walking. It may take you from one place to another, but so does crawling, and you outgrew that ages ago. Walking briskly does marvelous things for your health, your appearance and your mood—you can't stay sad or angry when you're moving along at a lively pace. It also tells people that you're really going some place, even if it's only to the corner for a loaf of bread.

Try this experiment: stand at a corner near school at dismissal time and watch the boys and girls as they walk along. Without glancing at faces, try to pick out those whose walk makes them look as if they'd be fun to know and spend time with. See how much you can learn about a person just from the way she or he walks? Don't you want your walk to say good things about you, too?

Then start picking up your feet instead of dragging them. Walk purposefully instead of aimlessly meandering. Hold your head up, take deep breaths and swing your arms. Surprisingly, you'll be less tired after walking this way than after slouching along, and you will cover more ground faster. And it's excellent exercise as well!

EXERCISES TO HIT THE SPOT

If improving your posture doesn't do enough to flatten your tummy, there are exercises that will. But you have to do them regularly and you have to be patient—there will be no instant results. It usually takes a couple of months of regular daily exercising before you notice any change.

Before doing exercises, it's important to do at least some stretching or warm-ups to make sure you don't pull or strain any muscles. So begin by standing with your feet comfortably apart and bend forward from the waist with the arms, head and neck completely relaxed. Slowly reach lower and lower until your fingertips touch the floor. You may not be able to reach that far the first day or even the first week but that's okay; eventually you will. Next, lie on the floor on your side and raise your leg till your toes point to the ceiling. Turn

[68]

over and raise the other leg. Now that you've stretched, you can start other exercises.

To tighten your tummy, lie flat on the floor on your back with your arms at your sides and your feet together. Slowly raise your legs, keeping your knees straight, until your legs are at a right angle to your torso. Then, very slowly, lower your legs to the floor. Rest for a count of five, then repeat the exercise. Breathe *in* as you raise your legs and *out* as you lower them. Do this three times the first day, adding another time each day until you are doing ten a day. It's important that you raise and lower your legs as slowly as possible. In addition to strengthening your stomach muscles, this exercise is also good for your thighs.

Sit-ups are another good way to tighten the stomach muscles. Lie on your back with your knees bent and your arms folded across your chest. Have someone hold your ankles or put your feet under the edge of a heavy piece of furniture so they can't lift more than an inch or two. Now raise your body to a sitting position, then slowly lower it back down to the floor. Breathe *in* as you sit up and *out* as you lie down. Do two or three sit-ups the first day, then gradually work your way up to ten. By then you probably won't need to anchor your ankles.

If you do this exercise with your legs straight, you'll tone up your leg muscles. You might want to alternate straight-leg sit-ups with bent-leg ones.

Here's an exercise to help you trim your thighs. Lie face down on the floor and bend your legs up from the knees. Reach back with your right

*Left: stretch every muscle before
you run, jog, or start an aerobics
class. Above: team sports offer
exercise and challenge.*

hand and grasp your right foot or ankle; do the same with your left hand and foot. Now raise your head, neck and upper body and gently rock back and forth four times. Relax and repeat the exercise. Do this three times the first day and add another each day until you're up to ten.

Exercising is fun when you do it to music. It's even more fun when you do it with friends. Many Y's have classes in aerobics that aren't expensive, and it's an excellent way to exercise and enjoy it. Tap and ballet dancing are also great ways to exercise, and of course there are sports. Soccer gives your legs a fine workout and tennis is terrific for the arms. Swimming exercises your arms and legs, and if you really stretch your arms in an overhead stroke, you'll also give your stomach muscles a good stretch.

You can even combine exercising with household chores. When you vacuum your room, for example, stretch your arms, bend from the waist and stand on one leg, raising the other out behind you. Stand on tiptoe and stretch as high as you can to dust high shelves instead of climbing on a ladder.

If you make exercise a part of your daily routine, you won't ever have to worry about flabby muscles!

PAINT AND POWDER

To many girls, wearing makeup means being grown up. It's something you're eager to do, and in your eagerness you may start using makeup before you need it and before you've learned to apply it properly. Some women wear makeup to highlight their good features, and occasionally, to play down less attractive ones. It is not used to cover up a dirty face or to disguise you with a "new" face. In fact, the woman who really knows how to apply makeup properly often looks as if she's not wearing much more than lipstick.

Many women prefer not to use makeup at all; certainly there's no law that says you have to. It takes time to put it on right, and the less you wear the less time you need to spend on your face. Natural is the important word in the way you look, and no one, regardless of age, looks natural with a lot of makeup on her face. And while you may not believe it, you will never look as good naturally as you do in your teens, so it doesn't make sense to cover your face with a lot of makeup.

You can learn a lot about the do's and don'ts of makeup by looking at the people you see every day. Your friends and classmates who plaster their faces with thick layers of foundation, blusher, eye shadow, mascara and eyeliner can look ridiculous. Before you appear in any sort of makeup, practice in private until you really know how to apply it well. Remember, too, that you don't need every type of cosmetic every day.

While you may see eleven-year-olds wearing some types of makeup, most girls—and their parents!—realize that it just doesn't look right on such young faces. Instead of making them look sophisticated, it just makes them look silly. At thirteen or fourteen, most girls start wearing lipstick and, depending upon their individual coloring, a light touch of blusher and perhaps some eye makeup.

When you think you're ready for makeup and your parents agree, the first thing you have to decide is what shades are most flattering for you. It doesn't matter what colors your best friend wears— she may be a pale-skinned blonde while you're an olive-skinned brunette. Obviously the same shades can't be right for both of you. When you think makeup, think natural. The idea is to look like yourself, not a painted doll.

In lipsticks, pure pinks, peaches and corals are usually best. The blue-reds—those with a hint of

*Take time to find the right
lipstick color for you.*

purple in them—rarely look good. Before buying a lipstick, test it on the back of your hand. Cosmetic counters often have testers that allow you to try before you buy; take advantage of that.

Foundations, which are also called makeup bases or simply makeup, should be as natural-looking as possible. They come in a wide variety of shades because people come in a wide variety of colors. Again, test before you buy. Select a shade that is only a little bit darker than your own complexion. Foundations that are lighter will make you look odd because your face won't match the rest of your skin. Follow this rule when buying powder, too.

Blushers can add a healthy-looking touch of color. They are available in many shades, and you should choose one that suits you. If your lipstick is a shade of peach, a blusher in peach rather than a pink or red shade works better. Of course, it's not necessary to match lipstick and blusher exactly.

If your eyebrows are so pale they can't be seen, you might want to darken them a little with an eyebrow pencil. Choose a color similar to your hair—auburn for red hair, light brown for blonde.

Eye shadow is another popular cosmetic but few young girls need it or take the time to apply it correctly. It's better to save it for special occasions. It comes in dozens of colors, and finding the shades that are best for you is often a matter of trial and error. This can be expensive!

Mascara and eyeliners should be in a shade that complements your own coloring. Dark-haired girls seldom need any, but blondes and redheads often have such pale lashes that they are almost invisible. If you have blonde eyelashes, black or dark brown mascara and eyeliner are too harsh for you; a light or medium brown is much better. But regardless of your coloring, stick to natural eyelash colors of brown or black instead of blues, greens or violets.

Remember to practice putting on makeup at home or with friends before wearing it in public. Keep in mind, too, that you don't have to wear makeup at all, and many young girls look better without it.

Cosmetics should always be applied lightly; don't plaster them on! For school, lipstick and a touch of blusher are usually enough if you decide to wear makeup at all. Save foundation and eye makeup for special occasions. That doesn't mean you should then smear eye shadow from eyelid to eyebrow because you're going to a party. Remember, the idea is to look as *un*made up as possible.

Makeup should be applied only to a clean face, and every bit of it needs to be removed at bedtime. Sleeping in makeup isn't good for your skin, so take the time to wash your face thoroughly before going to bed. If you wear a waterproof mascara, it can be removed with products sold for that purpose. Or you can use cold cream, petroleum jelly or baby oil to remove eye makeup and then

Practice putting on makeup
before you wear it in public.

wash your face with your regular soap and water. Pay special attention to the eye area so that you wash off all the cold cream or oil along with the traces of makeup.

Properly used, makeup won't harm normal skin, but some girls may find they are sensitive to certain brands. If your eyelids swell and itch when you use an eyeliner, for instance, stop using it immediately. This is true of all kinds of makeup; at the first sign of irritation, stop using it! Wait until the affected area is back to normal before trying another brand.

It is also not a good idea to share eye makeup with your friends. It's too easy to spread eye infections. And if you wear contact lenses, you need to be especially careful as some products may cause eye irritations.

Lipstick should be applied carefully, following the natural line of your lips. Don't try to make thin lips look fuller by going beyond the lips; that merely looks messy.

Foundation, if you wear it, should be applied sparingly all over your face, including the forehead and throat. Select a shade that is just a bit darker than your own complexion. Smooth it evenly to avoid a blotchy look. But if you have an acne problem, you'd be wise not to wear a foundation because it may clog your pores even more.

Blusher is for cheeks, and that's the only place to apply it. You may have enough color in your cheeks naturally so you don't need any, but sometimes—when you have your period, for example—you might look a little pale. When you put on a blusher, blend it in well so you don't leave a circle of color on your cheeks. Powder, either pressed or loose, goes on with a puff. Wash the puff often, or use a cotton ball and throw it away after each use. Again, the shade of powder should be close to your own complexion and it should be applied lightly.

Eyeliners come in pencil-like applicators, in liquids or in cakes that are applied with a brush; you need a steady hand to apply them. The pencil liners give a softer, more natural look. Draw a thin line close to the lashes on the upper lid and under the lashes on the lower lid. Blend in the lines to soften the look.

Mascara is applied from the roots of the lashes to the ends. And it should be applied only once; it's not necessary to add more during the day. Generally, the only makeup that needs touching up is lipstick and powder. The rest is applied at home and forgotten about until it's time to re-move it.

It can't be emphasized too strongly that a lot of makeup on a young face—or even an old one!—is a mistake in grooming. You can save time and money by putting your best face forward, and that's your natural face at the height of its youthful vi-tality.

Sunscreen is a different kind of cosmetic. Your skin needs protection from the sun whatever your skin color and whether you wear makeup or not. When you're going out in the sun, you should protect your face and all exposed areas of your skin with a good sunscreen. The labels on most suntan preparations have numbers; the higher the number, the more protection from the harmful burning rays of the sun. And you need that protection winter and summer, on the tennis court, on ski slopes, at a picnic in the park or when walking or jogging, just as much as you need it at the beach or pool.

THE
TOTAL
YOU

Now that you've learned how to groom yourself and have thought about dressing and applying makeup if you want to, it's time to think about the total you. Good grooming, like beauty, is more than skin deep. You can be the best-groomed girl in school but if you're inconsiderate, in the habit of cursing and being rude, you'll find yourself with fewer and fewer friends.

Not many things can ruin a good impression faster than bad language. Despite what you may hear in movies and on television, and in spite of the kind of language some adults may use, cursing is not a sign of sophistication or maturity. At best, it indicates a very limited vocabulary; at worst it shows you to be ill-bred and uncouth.

You have nothing to gain and a lot to lose by cursing. If you're in the habit of using foul language, stop it before it becomes too strong. And if your friends curse, remember that you don't have to do everything they do.

Do you think good manners are only to be used with adults? Then you're doing yourself and your friends a disservice. You don't have to be as formal with your friends as you are with the school principal, but "please" and "thank you" are appreciated by young and old alike.

If you had an appointment with your aunt to go shopping and something delayed you, you would call to let her know you'd be late. But do you extend the same courtesy to a friend? You should, because being considerate of others is an important part of the total you.

Keeping your word to your friends is a good habit, too. For instance, if you have a date with a friend to go to the movies and something better comes along, would you break the date? How would you feel if Sue broke a date with you to do something else? There will be times when the situation is beyond your control and you'll have to disappoint a friend, but be honest about it. Tell Sue or Alan that a family emergency has come up or that your cold is worse or whatever. Friends can understand that, but the casually broken date will eventually mean fewer and fewer dates.

Good manners aren't old-fashioned; they're needed every day to make life run a little more smoothly. Even though your friends may not mention it, they, too, like to be treated with thoughtfulness and consideration.

LET'S
PARTY!

One of the nicest things about going to a party or to a school dance is the fun of getting ready for it. Even if the party is an informal get-together at a friend's house or the dance is the usual Friday-night event, you'll enjoy it more if you're dressed for it.

Are pants the order of the day? That's fine, but don't wear your tired old jeans and a faded T-shirt. Put on a decent pair of pants or jeans and a clean, attractive top. Make sure your hair is shining clean and that the rest of you passes your personal inspection with flying colors. Add an attractive scarf or a string of beads to your outfit. These little touches help to put you in a party mood, and also tell your host that you think enough of her or him to wear something special.

There's another reason why dressing up for special occasions is a good idea. A school dance or a friend's party can be a shattering experience. But when you are confident about the way you look, you'll be much less nervous and can relax and enjoy yourself. Knowing you look your best goes a long way to help you face new and difficult situations bravely. That's the whole secret of the "why" of good grooming: to make your life easier by having one less thing—your appearance—to worry about.

So, before a party, allow yourself enough time to get ready. Start with a shower and shampoo your hair. If you use cosmetics, apply them lightly and properly. Give some thought to what you're going to wear. Is it suitable for the occasion? You don't want to be overdressed, but you don't want to look like a slob, either.

Is a friend, boy or girl, coming by to pick you up for the party? Then make sure you're ready on time. Keeping someone waiting is inconsiderate; being late is the same as telling your friend that you don't think much of her or him.

Go off to the party, confident that you look your best. Have a good time, but keep an eye on the clock. Getting home when you're supposed to may not have anything to do with good grooming, but it's an excellent way to show your parents that you are mature enough to follow the rules. And that can lead to your being allowed more freedom.

*Extra touches help to
put you in a party mood.*

*Clean, healthy and well-groomed
—you're ready for any party.*

At first glance, good grooming may seem like a lot of work, but it really isn't. Like everything else, the more you practice it, the easier it becomes. Besides, you won't have to go through the entire head-to-toe routine every single day. But it's never too early to learn how to take care of yourself and your clothes; before you know it, you'll be away from home and no one will be there to remind you to comb your hair or to pick up your sweater. So start now learning how to become the well-groomed young woman you want to be.

GOOD GROOMING CHECKLIST

Every Day

Morning
- ☐ Thoroughly wash your face and hands; brush and floss your teeth.
- ☐ Shower or take a bath (this can be done at bedtime if you prefer) and apply deodorant.
- ☐ Put on fresh underwear and clean clothes.
- ☐ Comb and brush your hair.

Noon
- ☐ Give your face another good washing and brush and floss your teeth, if possible.
- ☐ Check hair; does it need combing?

Night
- ☐ Bathe or shower (unless you've chosen the morning for this).

- Wash face thoroughly.
- Brush and floss teeth.
- Plan what you'll wear tomorrow.

Twice a Week
- Shampoo hair thoroughly (oily hair will require more frequent shampooing).

Once a Week
- Check fingernails and toenails; do they need cutting? Is your nail polish chipped?
- Check clothes for missing buttons, falling hems, spots or other problems. See that clothes are laundered or taken to the cleaner.

For Further
Reading

To learn more about the subjects covered in *Good Grooming for Girls,* look for these books in your school or public library:

Abrams, Joy, Ruth Richards, and Pam Gray. *Look Good, Feel Good: Through Yoga, Grooming, Nutrition.* New York: Holt, Rinehart and Winston, 1978.

Arnold, Caroline. *Too Fat? Too Thin? Do You Have a Choice?* New York: Morrow, 1984.

Eagles, Douglas, *Your Weight.* New York, Franklin Watts, 1982.

Gilbert, Sara. *Fat Free: Common Sense for Young Weight Worriers.* New York: Macmillan, 1975.

————. *You Are What You Eat.* New York: Macmillan, 1977.

Jacobs, Karen. *Health.* Chicago: Children's Press, 1981.

Kiss, Michaeline. *Yoga for Young People*. Indianapolis: Bobbs-Merrill, 1971.

LeMaster, Leslie Jean. *Nutrition*. Chicago: Children's Press, 1985.

Lewis, Nancy. *Keeping in Shape*. New York: Franklin Watts, 1976.

Long, Patricia. *The Nutritional Ages of Women*. New York: Macmillan, 1986.

Miller, Melba. *The Black Is Beautiful Beauty Book*. Englewood Cliffs: Prentice-Hall, 1974.

Neff, Fred. *Keeping Fit*. Minneapolis: Lerner Publications, 1977.

Novick, Nelson Lee, M.D. *Skin Care for Teens*. New York: Franklin Watts, 1988.

Peavy, Linda, and Smith, Ursula. *Food, Nutrition and You*. New York: Scribners, 1982.

Pinkham, Mary Ellen. *How to Become a Healthier and Prettier You*. New York: Doubleday, 1984.

Index

About the Author

Rubie Saunders has been deeply involved in the writing and editing of books and magazines for young readers all of her professional life.

She has written more than one hundred and fifty articles and a dozen books, including *The Concise Guide to Baby Sitting*.

A graduate of Hunter College in New York City, she was elected to the Hunter Hall of Fame. She enjoys working with youngsters and has received a distinguished service award from Cub Scout Pack 371 in Brooklyn.

She now lives in New Rochelle, New York, where she serves on the Board of Education.